Puglia Travel Guide

Discover the Secrets, Natural Treasures, and Traditional Foods of Puglia's Heritage with This Collection of Stories, Travel Itineraries and Over 50 Local Contacts

Lucy Evans

Contents

Introduction   **7**
Discovering Puglia: A Land of Contrasts 7
A Journey Through Time: Puglia's Rich History 8
Unveiling Puglia's Cultural Tapestry 10
From Coast to Countryside: Puglia's Diverse Landscapes . . . 11
Embracing Puglia's Culinary Delights 12

1   Chapter 1: Cities and Historical Monuments   **14**
  1.1   Foggia 14
  1.2   San Giovanni Rotondo 16
  1.3   Monte Sant'Angelo 18
  1.4   Bari 20
  1.5   Margherita di Savoia 22
  1.6   Alberobello 24
  1.7   Polignano a Mare 26
  1.8   Gioia Del Colle 28
  1.9   Taranto 30
  1.10 Lecce 32
  1.11 Otranto 34
  1.12 Gallipoli 36
  1.13 Santa Maria di Leuca 38

2   Chapter 2: Natural Splendor of Puglia   **40**
  2.1   Vieste and Pizzomunno 40
  2.2   Parco Nazionale del Gargano and Foresta Umbra 42
  2.3   Porto Cesareo 44
  2.4   Santa Maria al Bagno and Santa Caterina 46
  2.5   Porto Selvaggio 48
  2.6   Grotta del Drago 50
  2.7   Faraglioni di Sant'Andrea 52
  2.8   Grotta Verde di Andrano 54
  2.9   Cava di Bauxite 56

3   Chapter 3: The Most Iconic Pugliese Foods   **58**

3.1   Taieddrha 58

3.2   Panzerotto and Calzone 59

3.3   Mozzarella Fior di Latte 60

3.4   Panino con i Pezzetti di Cavallo 61

3.5   Polpo a Pignata 62

3.6   Peperoni Sott'Aceto con Pangrattato 63

3.7   Cozze Crude and Ricci di Mare 63

3.8   Orecchiette con Cime di Rape 65

4   Chapter 4: The Finest Selection of Wines   66

4.1   Salice Salentino 66

4.2   Primitivo di Manduria 67

4.3   Nero di Troia 68

4.4   Castel del Monte Rosso Riserva 68

4.5   Bombino Bianco 69

4.6   Negroamaro 70

Conclusion and Bonus   71

Grab Your Free Bonuses!   73

List of Figures

1.1 Piazza XX Settembre, Foggia 14
1.2 Cathedral "Beata Maria Vergine Assunta in Cielo" 15
1.3 Chiesa in San Giovanni Rotondo 16
1.4 A detail of the church of San Giovanni Rotondo 17
1.5 Castel of Monte Sant'Angelo 18
1.6 Inner Sanctorum Monte Sant'Angelo 19
1.7 Lungomare di Bari 20
1.8 The Red of Margherita di Savoia 22
1.9 Trulli of Alberobello 24
1.10 Grotta Palazzese, Polignano a Mare 26
1.11 The Beach in Polignano a Mare 27
1.12 The Castle of Gioia del Colle 28
1.13 The Sea of Taranto 30
1.14 Piazza Duomo in Lecce Over Night 32
1.15 Otranto, The Hidden Treasure of Puglia 34
1.16 The Castle and the Sea of Gallipoli 36

2.1 Vieste from the Sea 40
2.2 The Rock of Pizzomunno 41
2.3 Gargano Natural Parc 42
2.4 Foresta Umbra 43
2.5 The "Lungomare" of Porto Cesareo 44
2.6 The protected area of Porto Cesareo 45
2.7 Santa Caterina Centre over Night 46
2.8 A Typical Sunset in Santa Caterina 47
2.9 The Torre D'Alto In Porto Selvaggio 48
2.10 The Sun hits Porto Selvaggio 49
2.11 Grotta del Drago, Santa Maria di Leuca 50
2.12 The Cliff of the West Pugliese Coast 51
2.13 Faraglioni di Sant'Andrea from the Sea 52
2.14 Faraglioni di Sant'Andrea from the Cliff 53
2.15 The Green Cave, Andrano 54
2.16 Inside the Green Cave, Andrano 55
2.17 The Wonderful Cava di Bauxite close to Castro and Otranto 56
2.18 The Vivid Red of the Bauxite 57

3.1   Calzone (Lecce) or Panzerotto (elsewhere) 59
3.2   Panino con Pezzetti di Cavallo al Sugo 61
3.3   Cooking Octopus 62
3.4   The Famous Ricci di Mare 64
3.5   Orecchiette con Cime di Rapa 65

4.1   One of Finest Primitivo di Manduria 67
4.2   A Typical Picture of Wine in Glass during Summer 70

Introduction

Nestled in the sun-drenched heel of Italy's boot lies a land of enchantment and discovery: Puglia. Known for its whitewashed villages perched atop cliffs, olive groves stretching endlessly towards the horizon, and a coastline that shifts from rugged cliffs to golden sands, Puglia captivates the heart and soul of all who wander its storied landscapes.

Steeped in millennia of history, Puglia is a testament to resilience and adaptation. Its strategic position on the Mediterranean has made it a coveted prize for empires and civilizations throughout the ages, each leaving their mark on its rich cultural tapestry. From the ancient Greeks who settled its shores to the Byzantine monks who carved sanctuaries into its rocky cliffs, Puglia's history is etched into its architecture, cuisine, and way of life.

But Puglia is more than a living museum of history; it is a vibrant tapestry of traditions and modernity. Its people, with their warm hospitality and zest for life, welcome visitors into a world where ancient rituals blend seamlessly with contemporary culture. Whether wandering through the labyrinthine streets of Lecce's baroque old town or savoring the simplicity of a homemade pasta dish in a family-run trattoria, every moment in Puglia is an invitation to immerse oneself in its unique charm and beauty.

Join us on a journey through Puglia's diverse landscapes, where every turn reveals a new chapter in its storied past and a glimpse into its promising future. From the bustling ports of Bari and Brindisi to the tranquil olive groves of the Valle d'Itria, Puglia beckons with its timeless allure and promises an unforgettable adventure for those who dare to explore its depths.

Discovering Puglia: A Land of Contrasts

Puglia, often called Italy's best-kept secret, is a land of breathtaking contrasts that captivates the heart and soul of every traveler fortunate enough to explore its shores. Nestled in the heel of Italy's boot, this region boasts sun-kissed coastlines with azure waters that shimmer under the Mediterranean sun. Each town and village tells its own story through winding streets adorned with whitewashed buildings and vibrant bougainvillea cascading down ancient stone walls.

But Puglia is more than just its scenic beauty; it's a place where history whispers through the centuries-old olive groves and vineyards that blanket its countryside. The air is perfumed with the scent of centuries-old olive trees, standing as silent witnesses to the region's past. Traces of ancient civilizations, from the Greeks to the Romans and Byzantines, dot the landscape, reminding visitors of Puglia's rich cultural heritage and storied past.

Yet, amidst this historical tapestry, Puglia pulses with a vibrant energy and warmth that welcomes travelers like old friends. The hospitality of its people, expressed through hearty laughs and traditional feasts shared around sun-dappled tables, leaves an indelible mark on those who visit. From the bustling markets overflowing with fresh produce and artisanal crafts to the lively festivals that echo with music and laughter, Puglia invites you to embrace life's simple pleasures and forge connections that transcend language and borders.

To discover Puglia is to embark on a journey of contrasts—where ancient traditions meet modern delights, where serene landscapes meet bustling towns, and where the timeless allure of the Mediterranean meets the vibrant spirit of Italian life. Whether wandering through olive groves that stretch to the horizon or savoring the flavors of freshly caught seafood by the sea, Puglia beckons you to slow down, savor the moment, and immerse yourself in its beauty and charm.

Come, let Puglia enchant you with its contrasts, and leave with memories that linger long after you've bid farewell to this extraordinary land.

A Journey Through Time: Puglia's Rich History

Puglia, steeped in the echoes of millennia, invites travelers on a profound journey through time, where each ancient stone and whispering olive grove tells a story of resilience, culture, and enduring beauty. From the rugged cliffs of the Gargano Peninsula to the sun-drenched plains of the Salento, Puglia's landscapes are a canvas on which history has painted its most vibrant tales.

The history of Puglia unfolds like a tapestry woven with threads of conquest, trade, and cultural exchange. It began with the mysterious Nuragic civilization, whose stone monuments still stand sentinel over the land. The Greeks followed, leaving behind majestic temples and the foundation of agricultural practices that thrive to this day. The Romans, with their engineering prowess, built cities and aqueducts that shaped urban life in ancient times.

But perhaps the most poignant chapters of Puglia's history are written in the Byzantine era, when the region became a beacon of art, spirituality, and learning. Monasteries perched atop rocky cliffs, such as those in Monte Sant'Angelo and Santa Maria di Leuca, became centers of religious devotion and cultural exchange. The enduring legacy of Saint Nicholas in Bari and the stunning mosaics of Otranto Cathedral bear witness to this golden age of Byzantine influence.

Through centuries of change and upheaval, Puglia emerged as a crossroads of civilizations, a place where East met West and North met South. Its strategic position in the Mediterranean made it a coveted prize for conquerors, yet its people have always maintained a fierce independence and resilience. They celebrate their heritage with festivals that blend pagan rituals with Christian traditions, such as the vibrant Tarantella dance festivals and the solemn processions of Holy Week.

Today, Puglia's rich history is preserved in its ancient cities, fortified castles, and archaeological sites that dot the landscape. Each visit to a historical monument, whether it's the imposing Castel del Monte or the baroque splendor of Lecce's churches, is an opportunity to connect with the past and marvel at the ingenuity of those who came before.

To journey through Puglia's history is to be transported through time, to walk in the footsteps of ancient peoples and witness the enduring legacy they left behind. It's a reminder that history is not just a series of events, but a living, breathing tapestry that continues to shape the identity and spirit of Puglia and its people.

Unveiling Puglia's Cultural Tapestry

Puglia, a land where every stone, every dish, and every tradition tells a story of resilience, creativity, and deep-rooted cultural heritage. To explore Puglia is to unravel a vibrant tapestry woven with centuries of traditions, where the past meets the present in a celebration of life, art, and community.

At the heart of Puglia's cultural tapestry are its people, whose warmth and hospitality embrace visitors like family. They proudly preserve ancient traditions passed down through generations, from the art of olive oil production in the gnarled groves of centuries-old trees to the craftsmanship of stone masons who carve intricate designs into the white limestone facades of Ostuni and Martina Franca.

Puglia's cultural richness extends beyond its landscapes to its cuisine, a symphony of flavors that reflects its agricultural bounty and culinary ingenuity. From the earthy simplicity of orecchiette pasta with cime di rapa to the delicate sweetness of pasticciotto pastries filled with custard, every dish tells a tale of local ingredients and time-honored techniques. The ritual of gathering around a table, sharing homemade wine and laughter, epitomizes the soulful connection between food, family, and community in Puglia.

The region's architecture is a testament to its storied past, with whitewashed villages clinging to cliffs overlooking the Adriatic Sea and imposing castles that once defended against invaders. Each city, from the Baroque splendor of Lecce's churches to the medieval fortresses of Trani and Castel del Monte, bears witness to the artistic brilliance and architectural marvels of Puglia's past civilizations.

Artistry flourishes in Puglia's vibrant festivals and celebrations, where music, dance, and religious devotion intertwine in colorful processions and lively tarantella dances. From the mystical allure of the Grotto of Castellana to the spiritual sanctuaries of Monte Sant'Angelo and San Giovanni Rotondo, Puglia's sacred sites inspire reverence and reflection, offering pilgrims and travelers alike a profound connection to spiritual traditions that transcend time.

To unveil Puglia's cultural tapestry is to embark on a journey of discovery, where every encounter and every experience reveals a deeper understanding of the region's soul. It's a celebration of resilience, creativity, and the enduring spirit of a land that has shaped its identity through centuries of cultural exchange and artistic expression.

Come, immerse yourself in Puglia's cultural tapestry, and let its stories unfold before you, leaving an indelible mark on your heart and mind.

From Coast to Countryside: Puglia's Diverse Landscapes

Puglia unfolds like a masterpiece of nature's artistry, where each stroke of coastline, every rolling hill, and the whispering olive grove tells a tale of natural beauty and timeless tranquility. From the sun-drenched shores of the Adriatic Sea to the rugged cliffs of the Gargano Peninsula and the golden expanses of the Salento, Puglia's diverse landscapes beckon travelers to embark on a journey of discovery and wonder.

The coastline of Puglia is a mesmerizing tapestry of contrasts, where secluded coves and sandy beaches meet dramatic limestone cliffs and hidden sea caves. In places like Polignano a Mare and Santa Maria di Leuca, the turquoise waters of the Adriatic and Ionian Seas shimmer under the Mediterranean sun, inviting visitors to dip their toes into crystal-clear waters and lose themselves in the rhythmic melody of the waves.

Venture inland, and Puglia reveals a pastoral paradise dotted with ancient olive groves that stretch as far as the eye can see. These gnarled trees, some over a thousand years old, bear witness to the region's agricultural heritage and provide a serene backdrop for leisurely walks and contemplative moments. The countryside comes alive with the scent of wildflowers in spring, while the harvest season fills the air with the aroma of ripe figs and citrus fruits.

But Puglia's landscapes are more than just picturesque scenes; they are the essence of a way of life shaped by nature's bounty. The trulli of Alberobello and the masserie (farmhouses) scattered throughout the countryside speak to a tradition of rural living that honors simplicity and sustainability. Here, time seems to slow down, allowing travelers to reconnect with the rhythms of nature and appreciate the beauty of life's quiet moments.

From the ancient forests of the Gargano National Park to the fertile plains of the Tavoliere delle Puglie and the rocky cliffs of the Valle d'Itria, Puglia's diverse landscapes inspire awe and reverence. They are a testament to the region's resilience and the enduring bond between its people and the land they call home.

To journey from coast to countryside in Puglia is to embark on a voyage of the senses, where every vista, every scent, and every sound evokes a deep sense of connection to nature and the timeless beauty that surrounds us. It's an invitation to slow down, breathe in the fragrant air, and marvel at the wonders of a land that continues to captivate and enchant with its unparalleled landscapes.

Come, explore Puglia's diverse landscapes, and let their beauty touch your soul, leaving you forever changed by the magic of this extraordinary region.

Embracing Puglia's Culinary Delights

Puglia's culinary tradition is a feast for the senses, a symphony of flavors that celebrates the region's rich agricultural heritage, Mediterranean climate, and vibrant cultural tapestry. To savor Puglia's culinary delights is to embark on a journey of taste and tradition, where each dish tells a story of passion, ingenuity, and the timeless art of Italian cooking.

At the heart of Puglia's gastronomic identity lies its olive oil, affectionately known as "liquid gold." The ancient olive groves that blanket the countryside produce some of the finest olive oils in the world, each bottle a testament to generations of skill and dedication. From the peppery intensity of early harvest oils to the smooth, buttery notes of late harvest varieties, Puglia's olive oils elevate every dish they touch, from simple bruschetta to hearty orecchiette pasta.

No exploration of Puglia's cuisine is complete without indulging in its seafood bounty, freshly caught from the Adriatic and Ionian Seas. From delicate sea bream and red mullet to succulent octopus and tender cuttlefish, Puglia's coastal towns and fishing villages offer a tantalizing array of dishes that showcase the region's maritime heritage. Whether grilled to perfection, stewed in rich tomato sauce, or served raw in a refreshing seafood salad, each bite is a celebration of the sea's bounty and the skill of local fishermen.

Puglia's pasta traditions are equally captivating, with handmade orecchiette pasta taking center stage. Named for its ear-like shape, orecchiette is traditionally paired with cime di rapa (turnip tops) or a rich tomato and meat ragù, creating a harmonious blend of flavors that speaks to the region's agrarian roots. Each twist and turn of the pasta dough reflects the hands that lovingly knead and shape it, a testament to the artistry and craftsmanship that define Puglia's culinary landscape.

The region's cuisine is also a celebration of seasonal ingredients and traditional techniques passed down through generations. From the earthy goodness of fava beans and wild asparagus in spring to the sweet perfection of figs and almonds in summer, Puglia's markets overflow with seasonal treasures that inspire chefs and home cooks alike. Traditional recipes, such as the rustic tiella (a layered casserole of rice, potatoes, and mussels) and the delicate pasticciotto (a pastry filled with creamy custard), are beloved staples that evoke memories of family gatherings and festive occasions.

To embrace Puglia's culinary delights is to savor the essence of Italian hospitality, where every meal is an opportunity to forge connections and create cherished memories. Whether dining in a rustic trattoria nestled in a medieval village or enjoying a picnic on a sun-drenched beach, Puglia invites you to slow down, savor each bite, and revel in the simple pleasures of good food and good company.

Come, immerse yourself in Puglia's culinary heritage, and let its flavors transport you to a world where tradition meets innovation, and every meal is a celebration of life's abundance and the joy of sharing.

Chapter 1: Cities and Historical Monuments

1.1 Foggia

Foggia, the main city of the Tavoliere delle Puglie plain in northern Puglia, is known for its strategic location, agricultural heritage, and historical significance dating back to ancient times.

History of the City

Foggia's history traces back to Roman times when it was an important agricultural center known as "Fovea." Over the centuries, it grew into a thriving medieval city under the influence of various rulers, including the Normans and the Swabians. In the 18th century, Foggia experienced a period of economic and cultural expansion, marked by the development of its agricultural industry and the construction of notable buildings and palaces. Today, Foggia serves as a commercial and cultural hub, reflecting its rich history through its architecture and urban layout.

Figure 1.1: Piazza XX Settembre, Foggia

14

Historical Monuments

Foggia boasts several historical monuments that reflect its diverse cultural heritage. The Cathedral of Foggia, dedicated to the Assumption of the Virgin Mary, is a prominent landmark with its impressive Baroque facade and ornate interior. Nearby, the Palazzo Dogana, once a royal residence, now houses the Civic Museum of Foggia, displaying archaeological finds and artifacts from the region's past. The Teatro Giordano, an elegant theater built in the early 20th century, hosts performances ranging from opera to modern drama, showcasing Foggia's vibrant cultural scene.

Famous For

Foggia is renowned for its agricultural production, particularly wheat and olive oil, which have been staples of the local economy for centuries. The Tavoliere delle Puglie plain surrounding Foggia is one of Europe's largest wheat-growing regions, known for its fertile soil and favorable climate. Olive groves dot the landscape, producing high-quality olive oil that is a cornerstone of Puglian cuisine. Foggia's culinary traditions also include rustic dishes like "cavatelli" pasta with broccoli rabe and "caciocavallo" cheese, showcasing the region's agricultural bounty and culinary creativity.

Traditional Events

Foggia hosts several traditional events that celebrate its cultural heritage and agricultural roots. The Festa di Sant'Alberico, held in June, honors the city's patron saint with religious processions, music performances, and fireworks. During the annual Grain Festival, typically held in late summer, farmers gather to celebrate the wheat harvest with food tastings, agricultural displays, and traditional folk dances. The Festival of the Patron Saints, celebrated in September, pays tribute to Foggia's religious heritage with parades, concerts, and street festivities. These events offer visitors a chance to immerse themselves in Foggia's vibrant traditions and community spirit.

Figure 1.2: Cathedral "Beata Maria Vergine Assunta in Cielo"

1.2   San Giovanni Rotondo

San Giovanni Rotondo, a small town nestled in the Gargano Mountains of northern Puglia, is internationally renowned as the home of Saint Pio of Pietrelcina, commonly known as Padre Pio. It attracts millions of pilgrims and visitors each year seeking spiritual solace and healing at the sanctuary dedicated to this beloved saint.

History of the City

San Giovanni Rotondo's history is closely intertwined with the life and legacy of Padre Pio. Born Francesco Forgione in 1887, Padre Pio arrived in San Giovanni Rotondo in 1916 and spent most of his life here until his death in 1968. He gained fame for his stigmata, mystical experiences, and reputation for holiness, attracting followers from around the world. The construction of the Sanctuary of Saint Pio of Pietrelcina began shortly after his death and continues to expand today. The town's growth and development have been shaped by the influx of pilgrims and devotees, turning it into a center of spiritual pilgrimage and devotion.

Figure 1.3: Chiesa in San Giovanni Rotondo

Historical Monuments

San Giovanni Rotondo is dominated by the Sanctuary of Saint Pio of Pietrelcina, a monumental complex that includes the old church, the new church, the crypt where Padre Pio's remains lie, and the Padre

Pio Pilgrimage Church. The Sanctuary is a place of prayer, reflection, and worship, adorned with artworks and sculptures depicting the life of Padre Pio and scenes from the Bible. The Casa Sollievo della Sofferenza, a hospital founded by Padre Pio, stands as a testament to his humanitarian legacy and continues to provide medical care to thousands of patients each year. The town's streets are lined with statues, plaques, and memorials honoring Padre Pio's life and spiritual influence.

Famous For

San Giovanni Rotondo is famous for its association with Padre Pio, whose presence continues to deeply resonate with visitors seeking comfort, healing, and spiritual guidance. Pilgrims come to venerate his relics, attend Mass at the Sanctuary, and participate in devotional practices such as praying the Rosary and confession. The spiritual aura of San Giovanni Rotondo permeates every aspect of daily life, making it a place of pilgrimage for Catholics and seekers of faith worldwide.

Traditional Events

San Giovanni Rotondo hosts several traditional events that honor Padre Pio and celebrate its religious heritage. The Feast of Saint Pio, held on September 23rd, commemorates the saint's life and legacy with religious processions, Masses, and cultural performances. During Holy Week, the town observes solemn ceremonies marking the Passion of Christ, culminating in the Easter Sunday celebrations. Pilgrims often participate in spiritual retreats, seminars, and conferences held throughout the year, deepening their faith and connection to Padre Pio's teachings.

Figure 1.4: A detail of the church of San Giovanni Rotondo

1.3   Monte Sant'Angelo

Nestled in the Gargano National Park, Monte Sant'Angelo is a historic town steeped in spirituality and natural beauty. Perched atop Monte Gargano, it is renowned for its religious significance, medieval architecture, and picturesque landscapes.

History of the City

Monte Sant'Angelo's history is intertwined with its status as a major pilgrimage site. According to legend, in the 5th century, Archangel Michael appeared multiple times to a local bishop, indicating the location as a sacred site. This led to the establishment of the Sanctuary of Monte Sant'Angelo, one of the oldest Christian shrines in Europe and a UNESCO World Heritage site. Over the centuries, pilgrims have traveled here seeking healing and spiritual solace, contributing to the town's growth and development. Monte Sant'Angelo has been a crossroads of cultures, influenced by Byzantine, Norman, and Swabian rulers, each leaving their mark on its architecture and religious traditions.

Figure 1.5: Castel of Monte Sant'Angelo

Historical Monuments

Monte Sant'Angelo is dotted with historical monuments that reflect its religious and medieval past. The Sanctuary of Monte Sant'Angelo, perched on the edge of a cliff, is the town's most revered landmark. Its ancient cave-chapel, known as the Grotto of Saint Michael the Archangel, is a place of pilgrimage and prayer, adorned with votive offerings and religious artifacts. The Castle of Monte Sant'Angelo, built by the Normans in the 10th century, offers panoramic views of the town and surrounding countryside. The Church of San Pietro, with its Romanesque facade and medieval cloister, is another architectural gem that illustrates the town's spiritual and cultural significance.

Famous For

Monte Sant'Angelo is famous for its spiritual heritage and the Sanctuary of Saint Michael the Archangel, which draws visitors from around the world. The sanctuary's crypt, containing the sacred cave where Archangel Michael is said to have appeared, is a place of reverence and reflection. Pilgrims climb the Scalinata (Stairway of Wishes) to reach the sanctuary, seeking blessings and miracles. The town is also known for its traditional craftsmanship, particularly in woodworking and religious art. Local artisans produce intricate statues, crosses, and religious artifacts that are sold in shops throughout Monte Sant'Angelo.

Traditional Events

Monte Sant'Angelo hosts several traditional events that celebrate its religious and cultural heritage. The Feast of Saint Michael the Archangel, held on September 29th, is the town's most important celebration. Pilgrims and locals gather for religious processions, solemn masses, and cultural performances. During Holy Week, the town comes alive with ceremonies and processions marking the Passion of Christ. The Feast of Saint Leonard, in November, honors the town's patron saint with food, music, and festivities. These events offer a glimpse into Monte Sant'Angelo's deep-rooted traditions and community spirit.

Figure 1.6: Inner Sanctorum Monte Sant'Angelo

1.4 Bari

Bari, the bustling capital of Puglia, is a city that effortlessly blends history, culture, and modernity. With its vibrant street life, stunning seaside promenade, and rich cultural heritage, Bari offers a captivating experience for visitors.

Figure 1.7: Lungomare di Bari

History of the City

Bari's history dates back over two millennia, with its origins as an ancient Greek colony. It later became a significant Roman port and continued to thrive during the Byzantine era. The city gained prominence in the Middle Ages as a major center of trade and pilgrimage, particularly after the relics of Saint Nicholas were brought to Bari in 1087. These relics remain housed in the Basilica di San Nicola, making the city a vital religious destination. Bari's strategic coastal position has made it a crucial hub for maritime trade throughout its history, shaping its development and cultural landscape.

Historical Monuments

Bari is home to numerous historical monuments that reflect its diverse heritage. The Basilica di San Nicola, a masterpiece of Romanesque architecture, is a major pilgrimage site and houses the relics of Saint Nicholas. The Bari Cathedral, dedicated to Saint Sabinus, features a stunning blend of architectural styles from different periods. The Castello Normanno-Svevo, a formidable Norman-Swabian castle, stands as a testament to the city's medieval past and offers panoramic views of the old town. The historic center, known as Bari Vecchia, is a labyrinth of narrow alleys, ancient churches, and bustling piazzas that invite exploration and discovery.

Famous For

Bari is famous for its rich cultural scene and culinary delights. The city is renowned for its orecchiette pasta, often handmade by local women in the streets of Bari Vecchia. Bari's seafood is another highlight, with dishes like "riso, patate e cozze" (rice, potatoes, and mussels) and fresh raw fish being local specialties. The city's lively markets, such as the Mercato del Pesce and Mercato di Santa Scolastica, offer a sensory feast of sights, sounds, and flavors. Bari is also known for its vibrant festivals and traditions, reflecting its deep-rooted cultural heritage.

Traditional Events

Bari hosts several traditional events that celebrate its rich cultural and religious heritage. The Festa di San Nicola, held in May, is the city's most important celebration, featuring religious processions, historical reenactments, and a grand fireworks display over the sea. During Christmas, Bari Vecchia comes alive with festive lights, nativity scenes, and a bustling holiday market. The Fiera del Levante, an international trade fair held in September, showcases the region's economic and cultural achievements. These events offer a wonderful opportunity to experience the lively spirit and traditions of Bari.

Activities Nearby

The area surrounding Bari offers a variety of activities for visitors. The nearby town of Polignano a Mare, with its stunning cliffs and crystal-clear waters, is perfect for a day trip. The archaeological site of Egnazia, with its ancient ruins and museum, provides a fascinating glimpse into the region's past. The coastal town of Trani, known for its beautiful cathedral and picturesque harbor, is another must-visit destination. For those looking to relax, the beaches along the Adriatic coast offer sun, sea, and sand. Whether exploring historical sites, enjoying outdoor activities, or indulging in local cuisine, the area around Bari promises a memorable experience.

1.5 Margherita di Savoia

Margherita di Savoia, a coastal town in northern Puglia, is renowned for its therapeutic salt pans, sandy beaches, and natural beauty. Named after Queen Margherita of Savoy, this charming town offers visitors a unique blend of relaxation, history, and cultural richness.

Figure 1.8: The Red of Margherita di Savoia

History of the City

Margherita di Savoia's history is closely tied to its salt production industry, which dates back centuries. The town's salt pans, stretching along the Adriatic coast, have been in use since Roman times and were historically a major economic driver for the region. The discovery of ancient artifacts, including Roman pottery and coins, attests to the area's long-standing importance. Over the centuries, Margherita di Savoia evolved from a small fishing village into a popular seaside resort known for its therapeutic properties. Today, visitors can explore the salt museum to learn about the town's salt mining history and its impact on the local economy.

Historical Monuments

Margherita di Savoia is relatively modest in terms of historical monuments compared to other cities in Puglia. However, visitors can still discover some interesting landmarks. The Torre Imperiale, a coastal watchtower dating back to the 16th century, stands as a reminder of the town's defensive past. The Church of Santa Margherita, dedicated to the town's namesake, features a simple yet elegant Baroque facade and offers a peaceful retreat for reflection. The Museo della Civiltà del Mare showcases exhibits on local maritime traditions and artifacts recovered from shipwrecks off the coast.

Famous For

Margherita di Savoia is famous for its therapeutic salt pans, which are among the largest in Europe and are believed to have health benefits due to their high mineral content. The salt pans attract visitors seeking relaxation and wellness treatments, such as mud baths and salt scrubs, known for their healing properties. The town's sandy beaches, stretching for kilometers along the Adriatic coast, offer opportunities for sunbathing, swimming, and water sports. Margherita di Savoia is also renowned for its fresh seafood, with local dishes like "pesce azzurro" (bluefish) and "cozze alla marinara" (marinara mussels) being popular choices.

Traditional Events

Margherita di Savoia hosts several traditional events that celebrate its maritime heritage and cultural traditions. The Festa di Santa Margherita, held in July, honors the town's patron saint with religious processions, music, and fireworks. During the summer months, the town comes alive with festivals celebrating local cuisine, music, and arts. The Sagra del Pesce, a seafood festival, showcases the best of Margherita di Savoia's culinary delights, with fresh fish dishes prepared by local chefs. These events provide a wonderful opportunity for visitors to immerse themselves in the vibrant culture and community spirit of Margherita di Savoia.

Activities Nearby

The area surrounding Margherita di Savoia offers a variety of activities for nature enthusiasts and history buffs alike. The nearby Gargano National Park, with its rugged coastline and forested hills, is perfect for hiking, birdwatching, and exploring ancient cave dwellings. The town of Trani, known for its stunning cathedral and picturesque harbor, is a short drive away and offers a glimpse into medieval history. Wine enthusiasts can visit local vineyards to taste Puglia's renowned wines, such as Primitivo and Negroamaro. Whether relaxing on the beach, exploring historical sites, or indulging in local cuisine, Margherita di Savoia promises a memorable and enriching experience for all.

1.6   Alberobello

Alberobello, a UNESCO World Heritage site, is a unique and enchanting town in Puglia, famous for its distinctive trulli houses. These ancient, conical-roofed dwellings, made entirely of limestone, create a fairytale-like atmosphere that captivates visitors from around the world.

Figure 1.9: Trulli of Alberobello

History of the City

The history of Alberobello dates back to the 14th century when the first settlers, under the rule of the Counts of Conversano, built their homes using the dry stone technique to avoid paying taxes to the Kingdom of Naples. This method allowed for easy dismantling of the structures when inspections were announced. The town gradually developed, and by the late 18th century, it had grown significantly. In 1797, King Ferdinand IV of Bourbon granted Alberobello the status of a royal town, liberating it from feudal obligations. The town's unique architecture and historical significance have made it a cherished destination for those interested in history and culture.

Historical Monuments

Alberobello is renowned for its trulli, which are the town's most iconic historical monuments. The Rione Monti and Aia Piccola districts are home to over 1,500 trulli, each with its own unique character. The Trullo Sovrano, the largest trullo in Alberobello, is a must-visit, offering insight into the traditional way of life. The Church of Sant'Antonio, built in the shape of a trullo, is another architectural marvel. Additionally, the Trullo Siamese, with its two conjoined domes, stands out for its distinctive structure. Wandering through the narrow, winding streets lined with these ancient dwellings provides a glimpse into the town's rich architectural heritage.

Famous For

Alberobello is famous for its trulli, which are not found anywhere else in the world on such a scale. These unique structures, with their whitewashed walls and conical roofs, are a testament to the ingenuity and resourcefulness of the town's early inhabitants. Alberobello is also renowned for its artisanal crafts, particularly its handmade textiles and ceramics. The town's vibrant market scene offers a wide range of local products, from olive oil and wine to trulli-shaped souvenirs. The combination of its architectural uniqueness and rich cultural heritage makes Alberobello a standout destination in Puglia.

Traditional Events

Alberobello hosts several traditional events that celebrate its unique heritage and community spirit. The Festival of Saint Cosmas and Damian, the town's patron saints, takes place in September and features religious processions, music, and fireworks. During Christmas, the town transforms into a magical wonderland with a live nativity scene set among the trulli, attracting visitors from far and wide. In the summer, the streets come alive with festivals celebrating local food, music, and crafts. These events provide a wonderful opportunity to experience the vibrant culture and traditions of Alberobello.

1.7   Polignano a Mare

Polignano a Mare, perched dramatically on limestone cliffs overlooking the Adriatic Sea, is one of Puglia's most picturesque towns. Known for its stunning views, crystal-clear waters, and charming old town, Polignano a Mare offers a blend of natural beauty, history, and vibrant local culture.

Figure 1.10: Grotta Palazzese, Polignano a Mare

History of the City

Polignano a Mare's history stretches back to the ancient Greeks, who first established a settlement in the area. Later, it became a Roman colony, known as Neapolis, and flourished due to its strategic coastal location. The town's historic center, with its maze of narrow streets and whitewashed buildings, reflects its medieval past. Throughout the centuries, Polignano a Mare was influenced by various cultures, including the Normans and Byzantines, each leaving their mark on the town's architecture and cultural heritage.

Historical Monuments

Polignano a Mare boasts several historical monuments that tell the story of its rich past. The Roman Bridge, part of the ancient Via Traiana, stands as a testament to the town's Roman heritage. The Church of Santa Maria Assunta, located in the heart of the old town, features a beautiful blend of Romanesque and Baroque architecture. The remnants of the ancient city walls and watchtowers offer glimpses into the town's medieval fortifications. The Palazzese Cave, a natural sea grotto used since ancient times, highlights the town's unique geological features and historical significance.

Famous For

Polignano a Mare is famous for its breathtaking cliffs and sea caves, which create a stunning backdrop for the town. The pristine beaches and clear waters are ideal for swimming, snorkeling, and diving, attracting visitors from around the world. The town is also renowned for its vibrant food scene, particularly its seafood, with dishes like "polpo alla pignata" (octopus stew) and "ricci di mare" (sea urchins) being local specialties. Additionally, Polignano a Mare is the birthplace of the famous Italian singer Domenico Modugno, known for his iconic song "Volare," and his legacy is celebrated throughout the town.

Traditional Events

Polignano a Mare hosts a variety of traditional events that reflect its rich cultural heritage. The annual Red Bull Cliff Diving World Series, held at the dramatic Lama Monachile beach, draws athletes and spectators from around the globe. The Feast of San Vito, the town's patron saint, is celebrated in June with religious processions, fireworks, and street performances. During the summer, the town comes alive with music, dance, and food festivals, offering visitors a chance to experience the lively spirit and traditions of Polignano a Mare.

Figure 1.11: The Beach in Polignano a Mare

1.8   Gioia Del Colle

Gioia Del Colle, a charming town located in the heart of Puglia, is a place where history, culture, and gastronomy converge. Known for its rich historical heritage and as the birthplace of the renowned Primitivo wine, Gioia Del Colle offers visitors a unique and authentic experience of Southern Italy.

Figure 1.12: The Castle of Gioia del Colle

History of the City

The history of Gioia Del Colle dates back to ancient times, with archaeological evidence suggesting human settlement as far back as the Bronze Age. The town's name is believed to derive from "Jovia," a term linked to the Roman god Jupiter, reflecting its ancient roots. Throughout the Middle Ages, Gioia Del Colle flourished under the rule of various feudal lords, most notably the Norman Count Riccardo Siniscalco who built the imposing castle that dominates the town. The town's strategic location made it a significant agricultural and trade center, contributing to its growth and prosperity over the centuries.

Historical Monuments

Gioia Del Colle is home to several historical monuments that showcase its rich cultural heritage. The Castello Normanno-Svevo, a magnificent Norman-Swabian castle, stands as a symbol of the town's medieval past.

This well-preserved fortress offers stunning views of the surrounding countryside and houses a museum that provides insights into the town's history. The Chiesa Madre, or Mother Church, dedicated to Santa Maria Maggiore, features beautiful Baroque architecture and intricate frescoes. The town's historic center, with its narrow streets and ancient buildings, invites visitors to explore and discover its hidden treasures.

Famous For

Gioia Del Colle is famous for its production of Primitivo wine, one of Puglia's most celebrated varietals. The town's vineyards benefit from the region's unique terroir, producing wines that are rich, robust, and full-bodied. Gioia Del Colle is also known for its delicious dairy products, particularly its mozzarella and burrata cheeses, which are highly regarded throughout Italy. The local cuisine, featuring traditional dishes made from fresh, locally-sourced ingredients, is another highlight, offering a true taste of Pugliese culinary traditions.

Traditional Events

Gioia Del Colle's cultural calendar is filled with traditional events that reflect its vibrant community spirit. The Festa di San Filippo Neri, held in May, is a major religious celebration featuring processions, fireworks, and various cultural activities. The Sagra della Mozzarella, a festival dedicated to the town's famous cheese, attracts food lovers with tastings, demonstrations, and live music. Throughout the year, various fairs, markets, and festivals take place, celebrating everything from local crafts to agricultural products, and providing visitors with a glimpse into the town's lively traditions and warm hospitality.

Activities Nearby

The area surrounding Gioia Del Colle offers a variety of activities for visitors to enjoy. The nearby Alta Murgia National Park provides opportunities for hiking, cycling, and wildlife spotting amidst stunning natural landscapes. The ancient town of Matera, with its famous Sassi cave dwellings, is just a short drive away and offers a fascinating glimpse into Italy's prehistoric past. For wine enthusiasts, touring the local vineyards and tasting the renowned Primitivo wines is a must. Whether exploring nature, history, or gastronomy, the activities near Gioia Del Colle ensure a memorable and enriching experience for all.

1.9 Taranto

Taranto, a historic city located on the Gulf of Taranto in the Ionian Sea, is known as the "City of the Two Seas" due to its unique position between the Mar Grande and the Mar Piccolo. With its rich history, diverse cultural heritage, and striking coastal landscapes, Taranto offers a fascinating blend of the ancient and the modern, making it a captivating destination in Puglia.

Figure 1.13: The Sea of Taranto

History of the City

The history of Taranto is deeply rooted in antiquity, dating back to its founding by Spartan settlers in 706 BC. Known as Taras in ancient times, it became one of the most important cities of Magna Graecia. Taranto flourished under Greek rule, becoming a major center of commerce and culture. Throughout its history, it has seen Roman conquest, Byzantine governance, and Norman rule, each era leaving its mark on the city's architecture and culture. The city's strategic naval position has also made it a significant military hub over the centuries, contributing to its rich and complex historical tapestry.

Historical Monuments

Taranto is home to numerous historical monuments that reflect its storied past. The Aragonese Castle, a formidable fortress built in the 15th century, stands guard at the entrance to the old town and offers panoramic views of the sea. The Cathedral of San Cataldo, with its stunning Baroque interior and Romanesque facade, is a testament to the city's religious and architectural heritage. The National Archaeological Museum of Taranto (MArTA) houses one of the most important collections of Greek and Roman artifacts in Italy, showcasing the city's ancient splendor. Additionally, the Ponte Girevole, a unique swing bridge, connects the old town to the new and symbolizes Taranto's blend of tradition and modernity.

Famous For

Taranto is famous for its rich maritime heritage and its status as a major naval base. The city's two seas, the Mar Grande and the Mar Piccolo, are renowned for their beauty and ecological significance, providing a unique marine environment. Taranto is also celebrated for its culinary traditions, particularly its seafood dishes, with local specialties like mussels from the Mar Piccolo and "cozze tarantine" being highly prized. The city's vibrant fish market, located in the old town, is a testament to its deep connection with the sea.

Traditional Events

Taranto's cultural calendar is rich with traditional events that highlight its deep-rooted heritage and vibrant community spirit. The Holy Week processions, known as "Settimana Santa," are among the most important in Italy, featuring solemn parades, religious ceremonies, and centuries-old traditions. The Feast of San Cataldo, the city's patron saint, is celebrated in May with processions, music, and festivities that bring the community together. The Palio di Taranto, a traditional rowing race held in the summer, showcases the city's maritime heritage and competitive spirit.

Activities Nearby

The area surrounding Taranto offers a wealth of activities for visitors to enjoy. The nearby beaches of the Ionian coast, such as Marina di Ginosa and Campomarino, are perfect for sunbathing and swimming. The Riserva Naturale Regionale Bosco delle Pianelle provides opportunities for hiking and birdwatching amidst beautiful natural landscapes. For history enthusiasts, the ancient city of Metaponto, with its well-preserved Greek temples and archaeological sites, is just a short drive away.

1.10 Lecce

Lecce, often referred to as the "Florence of the South," is a city renowned for its stunning Baroque architecture, rich cultural heritage, and vibrant atmosphere. Nestled in the heart of the Salento Peninsula, Lecce captivates visitors with its intricate facades, historic landmarks, and lively piazzas, offering a perfect blend of history, art, and modernity.

Figure 1.14: Piazza Duomo in Lecce Over Night

History of the City

Lecce's history spans more than two millennia, with roots tracing back to the Messapians, an ancient Italic tribe. It flourished under Roman rule, becoming an important center for trade and culture. During the Middle Ages, Lecce experienced periods of Byzantine, Norman, and Swabian influence, each leaving its mark on the city. However, it was during the Baroque period in the 17th century that Lecce truly blossomed, with the construction of numerous churches, palazzi, and public buildings adorned with elaborate stonework, earning the city its nickname.

Historical Monuments

Lecce is a treasure trove of historical monuments that reflect its rich architectural heritage. The Basilica di Santa Croce stands as a masterpiece of Baroque art, with its ornate facade and stunning rose window. The Piazza del Duomo is another highlight, featuring the Lecce Cathedral, the Bishop's Palace, and the Seminary, all showcasing the city's Baroque splendor. The Roman Amphitheatre, located in the heart of the city, offers a glimpse into Lecce's ancient past, while the Porta Napoli, an impressive triumphal arch, marks the entrance to the historic center. Wandering through Lecce's streets, visitors encounter countless other architectural gems that narrate the city's illustrious history.

Famous For

Lecce is famous for its distinctive Baroque architecture, characterized by intricate carvings and elaborate facades that adorn its churches and palazzi. The city's craftsmen have long been celebrated for their skill in working with the local pietra leccese, a soft limestone that allows for exquisite detailing. Lecce is also renowned for its vibrant cultural scene, with numerous festivals, art exhibitions, and live performances taking place throughout the year. The city's culinary traditions are equally notable, with local specialties such as "pasticciotto," a sweet pastry, and "ciceri e tria," a traditional pasta dish, delighting food enthusiasts.

Traditional Events

Lecce's cultural calendar is filled with traditional events that highlight its rich heritage and community spirit. The Festa di Sant'Oronzo, held in late August, is the city's most important celebration, honoring its patron saint with processions, fireworks, and street performances. The Fiera di Santa Lucia, a Christmas market featuring local crafts and nativity scenes, brings a festive atmosphere to the city in December. Throughout the year, Lecce hosts various festivals celebrating music, theater, and art, offering visitors a chance to immerse themselves in the city's lively and creative ambiance.

Activities Nearby

The surrounding area of Lecce offers a wealth of activities for visitors to explore. The nearby Adriatic coast boasts beautiful beaches such as Torre dell'Orso and Otranto, perfect for sunbathing and swimming. The historic town of Gallipoli, with its charming old town and stunning seaside views, is just a short drive away. For nature lovers, the Parco Naturale Regionale Costa Otr

1.11   Otranto

Otranto, the easternmost town in Italy, is a captivating blend of history, culture, and natural beauty. Perched on the Adriatic coast, this ancient city has witnessed the passage of numerous civilizations, each leaving its indelible mark on its landscape and heritage. With its turquoise waters, charming streets, and rich historical legacy, Otranto is a jewel of the Salento Peninsula.

Figure 1.15: Otranto, The Hidden Treasure of Puglia

History of the City

The history of Otranto is as deep and diverse as the Adriatic Sea it borders. Founded by the Greeks and later a prominent Roman port, Otranto has been a crucial maritime and trade hub for centuries. It was a significant stronghold during the Byzantine era and later under Norman rule. The town's strategic position made it a target for invasions, most notably by the Ottomans in 1480, who left a profound impact on its history. The resilience of Otranto's people is reflected in the city's enduring spirit and rich cultural tapestry.

Historical Monuments

Otranto is home to a wealth of historical monuments that narrate its storied past. The Otranto Cathedral, or Cattedrale di Santa Maria Annunziata, is renowned for its stunning mosaic floor, depicting the Tree of Life and various biblical scenes. The Aragonese Castle, a formidable fortress with panoramic views of the sea, stands as a testament to the town's strategic importance. Walking through Otranto's narrow, cobbled streets, visitors can discover the Byzantine Church of St. Peter, with its well-preserved frescoes, and the ancient city walls that have withstood the test of time.

Famous For

Otranto is famous for its picturesque coastal scenery and vibrant cultural heritage. The town's beaches, with their fine white sand and crystal-clear waters, are among the most beautiful in Puglia, attracting sun-seekers and water sports enthusiasts alike. Otranto's old town is a maze of charming alleys, lined with whitewashed houses, artisan shops, and bustling cafes. The town is also celebrated for its culinary delights, particularly its fresh seafood and traditional dishes like "pittule" and "orecchiette." Otranto's unique blend of history, culture, and natural beauty makes it a beloved destination for travelers.

Traditional Events

Otranto's cultural calendar is filled with traditional events that showcase its rich heritage and community spirit. The Festa dei Martiri di Otranto, held in August, commemorates the 800 martyrs who died during the Ottoman invasion, with processions, religious ceremonies, and historical reenactments. The Sagra del Pesce, a seafood festival, celebrates the town's maritime traditions with feasts, music, and dancing. Throughout the year, various festivals and events bring Otranto's streets to life, offering visitors a glimpse into the town's vibrant traditions and lively atmosphere.

Activities Nearby

The area surrounding Otranto offers a wealth of activities for visitors to enjoy. The nearby Alimini Lakes are perfect for nature lovers, with their diverse flora and fauna and opportunities for birdwatching and hiking. The Grotta della Poesia, a stunning natural pool carved into the limestone cliffs, invites swimmers to dive into its clear, azure waters. For history enthusiasts, the ancient town of Lecce, known as the "Florence of the South," is just a short drive away, offering a wealth of Baroque architecture and cultural treasures. Whether exploring natural wonders or delving into the region's rich history, the activities near Otranto ensure a memorable and enriching experience for all.

1.12 Gallipoli

Gallipoli, known as the "Pearl of the Ionian Sea," is a stunning coastal town on the western side of the Salento Peninsula. Its name, derived from the Greek word "Kallipolis," meaning "beautiful city," perfectly captures the essence of this charming destination, which is famed for its crystal-clear waters, rich history, and vibrant culture.

Figure 1.16: The Castle and the Sea of Gallipoli

History of the City

Gallipoli boasts a fascinating history that dates back to ancient times. Originally founded by the Greeks, it later became an important Roman port. Throughout the Middle Ages, Gallipoli was a coveted prize for various powers, including the Byzantines, Normans, and the Kingdom of Naples. The town's strategic position made it a hub of maritime trade and military defense. Its history is reflected in the mix of architectural styles that adorn the old town, from ancient fortifications to Baroque churches, each bearing witness to Gallipoli's storied past.

Historical Monuments

Gallipoli is home to numerous historical monuments that narrate its rich and diverse history. The Castello di Gallipoli, a robust fortress standing guard at the entrance to the old town, offers stunning views and a glimpse into the town's defensive past. The Cattedrale di Sant'Agata, a masterpiece of Baroque architecture, dominates the skyline with its intricate facade and ornate interiors. Wandering through the old town's narrow streets, visitors can discover ancient palazzi, like Palazzo Tafuri, and historic churches that tell the story of Gallipoli's evolution over the centuries.

Famous For

Gallipoli is renowned for its pristine beaches and crystal-clear waters, making it a favorite destination for sun-seekers and water enthusiasts. The old town, perched on an island and connected to the mainland by a 17th-century bridge, is famous for its charming labyrinth of alleys, whitewashed houses, and vibrant markets. Gallipoli is also celebrated for its seafood cuisine, with local specialties like "scapece," a marinated fish dish, and the fresh catches of the day served at waterfront trattorias. The town's lively nightlife, particularly during the summer months, attracts visitors from all over Italy and beyond.

Traditional Events

Gallipoli's cultural calendar is filled with traditional events that highlight its rich heritage and lively community spirit. The Festa di Santa Cristina, held in July, is one of the most important celebrations, featuring processions, fireworks, and local music. The Carnevale di Gallipoli is another highlight, with colorful parades, elaborate costumes, and festive activities that bring joy to residents and visitors alike. Throughout the year, various religious and secular festivals provide a window into the traditions and customs that define Gallipoli's unique character.

Activities Nearby

Beyond the town itself, the surrounding area offers a wealth of activities for visitors to enjoy. The nearby Baia Verde is a popular destination for beachgoers, known for its golden sands and turquoise waters. For nature lovers, the Parco Naturale Regionale Isola di Sant'Andrea e Litorale di Punta Pizzo offers hiking trails and birdwatching opportunities amidst stunning coastal landscapes. Boat trips from Gallipoli's harbor allow for exploration of the Ionian Sea's hidden coves and marine reserves. Whether it's a day of relaxation on the beach or an adventure through nature, the activities nearby ensure that every visit to Gallipoli is filled with memorable experiences.

1.13 Santa Maria di Leuca

Nestled at the southernmost tip of the Salento Peninsula, where the Adriatic and Ionian seas converge, Santa Maria di Leuca is a beacon of history, culture, and natural beauty. This picturesque town, often referred to as the "End of the Land," enchants visitors with its stunning landscapes, rich heritage, and vibrant traditions.

History of the City

Santa Maria di Leuca boasts a history as captivating as its coastal vistas. The town's origins date back to ancient times when it was a bustling harbor for Greek and Roman ships. Throughout the centuries, it has been a crossroads of various civilizations, including the Byzantines, Normans, and Saracens, each leaving their indelible mark on the region. The name "Leuca," meaning "white" in Greek, is believed to derive from the brilliant white limestone cliffs that frame the coastline, a striking feature that has guided sailors for millennia.

Historical Monuments

The historical monuments of Santa Maria di Leuca reflect its storied past and architectural grandeur. The Basilica Santuario di Santa Maria de Finibus Terrae stands as a testament to the town's spiritual significance, perched dramatically on a cliff overlooking the sea. This sacred site, originally a temple dedicated to Minerva, has been a place of pilgrimage since the Christian era. Nearby, the majestic lighthouse, one of Italy's tallest, offers panoramic views that stretch to the horizon, where myth and reality blend seamlessly. The intricate network of 19th-century villas, each with its unique style and history, adds to the town's charm, showcasing the opulence of the past aristocracy.

Famous For

Santa Maria di Leuca is renowned for its breathtaking natural beauty and serene ambiance. The town's pristine beaches, with their fine white sand and crystal-clear waters, are among the most beautiful in Puglia. It is also famous for the Grotte Marine, a series of sea caves accessible by boat, each with its unique geological formations and legends. The town's dual seascape, where the Ionian and Adriatic meet, creates a unique marine environment celebrated by divers and snorkelers alike. Moreover, Santa Maria di Leuca's rich culinary tradition, featuring fresh seafood and local delicacies, has earned it a reputation as a gastronomic haven.

Traditional Events

Santa Maria di Leuca is alive with vibrant traditions and cultural events that reflect its deep-rooted heritage. The Feast of Our Lady of Leuca, celebrated each August, is a highlight, featuring processions, fireworks, and local music that bring the community together in joyous celebration. The Festa del Mare, held in summer, showcases the town's maritime culture with boat parades, fishing competitions, and seafood feasts. Traditional Pizzica dances and folk music echo through the streets during festivals, offering visitors a glimpse into the heart of Salento's cultural tapestry.

Activities Nearby

Beyond its historical and cultural allure, Santa Maria di Leuca offers a plethora of activities for nature enthusiasts and adventure seekers. The coastal trails provide spectacular hiking opportunities, with paths leading to secluded beaches, hidden coves, and scenic viewpoints. Boat tours to the Grotte Marine allow for exploration of the stunning sea caves, while diving and snorkeling reveal the underwater treasures of the dual seas. Whether basking in the sun on its idyllic beaches or delving into its rich history, Santa Maria di Leuca promises an unforgettable experience at the "End of the Land."

Chapter 2: Natural Splendor of Puglia

2.1 Vieste and Pizzomunno

Description:

Perched on the dramatic Gargano Peninsula overlooking the Adriatic Sea, Vieste captivates with its whitewashed buildings clinging to cliffs, overlooking turquoise waters and golden beaches. At the heart of Vieste stands Pizzomunno, a towering limestone monolith rising majestically from the sandy shores. Legends abound about this natural wonder, said to have been a sailor transformed by love into stone, forever gazing out to sea.

Figure 2.1: Vieste from the Sea

How to find it:

Discovering Vieste and Pizzomunno is a journey through winding coastal roads that offer panoramic views of the Gargano coastline. Follow signs that lead you through narrow alleys lined with charming shops, cafes, and trattorias serving freshly caught seafood. As you approach the town, the scent of saltwater and Mediterranean herbs fills the air, guiding you to this picturesque seaside haven.

Activities Nearby:

In Vieste, embrace the coastal charm with leisurely walks along the waterfront promenade, offering stunning vistas of the Adriatic Sea and nearby islands. Explore hidden coves and sea caves by boat, discovering secluded beaches and crystal-clear waters perfect for swimming and snorkeling. Visit the historic Vieste Cathedral and Castle, where ancient stone walls and medieval architecture transport you back in time.

Special Stories From the Past:

Vieste and Pizzomunno have inspired myths and legends for centuries, woven into the fabric of local folklore and culture. Stories of mermaids and sea nymphs luring sailors to their depths mingle with tales of bravery and romance. Pizzomunno stands as a silent witness to these stories, its weathered facade bearing witness to the passage of time and the enduring spirit of the Gargano Peninsula. Today, Vieste remains a beloved destination where history and natural beauty converge, inviting travelers to explore

Figure 2.2: The Rock of Pizzomunno

2.2 Parco Nazionale del Gargano and Foresta Umbra

Description:

The Parco Nazionale del Gargano and Foresta Umbra form a pristine wilderness sanctuary nestled in the heart of Puglia. The Gargano Peninsula juts out into the Adriatic Sea, offering a diverse landscape of rugged cliffs, golden beaches, and lush forests. Foresta Umbra, in particular, captivates with its ancient beech and oak trees, creating a shaded canopy that filters sunlight onto moss-covered paths. The air is perfumed with the scent of wildflowers and resin, inviting visitors to explore its tranquil depths.

Figure 2.3: Gargano Natural Parc

How to find it:

Discovering the Parco Nazionale del Gargano and Foresta Umbra is a journey through winding mountain roads that offer panoramic views of the Adriatic coastline. Follow signs that lead you through picturesque villages and medieval towns perched on hilltops, where ancient stone walls and cobblestone streets whisper tales of centuries past. As you ascend into the forested hills of Gargano, the serenity of Foresta Umbra beckons, offering a retreat into nature's embrace.

Activities Nearby:

In the Parco Nazionale del Gargano, embrace the spirit of adventure with hiking trails that wind through dense forests and lead to hidden caves and cascading waterfalls. Discover secluded beaches and pristine coves along the coastline, perfect for sunbathing or swimming in the clear waters of the Adriatic. Explore historic sanctuaries and medieval castles that dot the landscape, offering glimpses into the region's rich cultural heritage and spiritual significance.

Special Stories From the Past:

The Parco Nazionale del Gargano and Foresta Umbra have been revered since ancient times for their natural beauty and spiritual significance. Legends speak of the Gargano Peninsula as a sacred place where Saint Michael the Archangel appeared, leaving behind a legacy of pilgrimage and devotion. Stories of mythical creatures and ancient rituals intertwine with the whispers of the wind through Foresta Umbra's ancient trees, creating a tapestry of folklore and wonder. Today, they remain sanctuaries of biodiversity and cultural heritage, inviting travelers to explore their hidden treasures and connect with the timeless rhythms of nature.

Figure 2.4: Foresta Umbra

2.3 Porto Cesareo

Description:

Nestled on the Ionian coast of Puglia, Porto Cesareo beckons with its pristine beaches, crystalline waters, and vibrant marine life. The azure sea stretches out like a vast mirror, reflecting the endless sky and the sun's golden rays. Soft, powdery sands embrace the coastline, inviting visitors to relax under the shade of swaying palm trees or indulge in leisurely walks along the water's edge. Lush Mediterranean vegetation frames the shores, creating a serene backdrop for this coastal paradise.

Figure 2.5: The "Lungomare" of Porto Cesareo

How to find it:

Discovering Porto Cesareo is a journey through coastal roads lined with olive groves and vineyards, offering glimpses of the sparkling sea beyond. Follow signs that lead you to this seaside haven, where the salty breeze and the rhythmic lullaby of waves guide you to its tranquil shores. Whether approaching by car or boat, the sight of Porto Cesareo's turquoise waters and picturesque harbor promises a sanctuary of relaxation and natural beauty.

Activities Nearby:

At Porto Cesareo, immerse yourself in the tranquility of its pristine waters with snorkeling or diving adventures to discover vibrant underwater ecosystems and ancient shipwrecks. Explore nearby islands and islets that dot the horizon, offering secluded beaches and panoramic views of the Ionian Sea. Indulge in freshly caught seafood at waterfront trattorias, where local delicacies are served with a side of warm hospitality and breathtaking sunset vistas.

Special Stories From the Past:

Porto Cesareo holds tales of ancient civilizations and maritime traditions that have shaped its coastal heritage. Legend has it that the waters surrounding Porto Cesareo were once traversed by Phoenician sailors and Roman galleys, leaving behind traces of their seafaring adventures. Today, it remains a cherished destination where stories of past and present intertwine, inviting travelers to explore its natural wonders and create cherished memories along its sun-kissed shores.

Figure 2.6: The protected area of Porto Cesareo

2.4 Santa Maria al Bagno and Santa Caterina

Description:

Nestled along the sun-drenched coastline of Puglia, Santa Maria al Bagno and Santa Caterina enchant visitors with their charming seaside allure. Santa Maria al Bagno boasts a crescent-shaped bay embraced by rugged cliffs and crystal-clear waters that shimmer under the Mediterranean sun. Quaint whitewashed buildings adorned with vibrant bougainvillea overlook the tranquil harbor, where colorful fishing boats bob gently in the tide. Just a short stroll away, Santa Caterina captivates with its picturesque harbor and panoramic views of the Adriatic Sea, framed by lush olive groves and citrus orchards that perfume the air with their sweet fragrance.

Figure 2.7: Santa Caterina Centre over Night

How to find them:

Discovering Santa Maria al Bagno and Santa Caterina is a journey through coastal roads that wind through ancient olive groves and vineyards. Follow signs that lead you through narrow streets lined with traditional trattorias offering freshly caught seafood and local delicacies. As you approach the seaside villages, the salty breeze and the sound of seagulls guide you to their tranquil shores, where time seems to stand still amidst their serene beauty.

Activities Nearby:

In Santa Maria al Bagno, indulge in the laid-back atmosphere with a refreshing swim in the azure waters or a leisurely sunbath on the golden sands of its beach. Explore coastal trails that offer stunning vistas of the Adriatic coast, perfect for capturing breathtaking sunset panoramas. In Santa Caterina, wander along the waterfront promenade, stopping at quaint cafes to savor freshly brewed espresso and local pastries. Engage in moments of tranquility as you absorb the timeless charm of these coastal villages, where the harmony of sea and land creates a captivating backdrop for unforgettable experiences.

Special Stories From the Past:

Santa Maria al Bagno and Santa Caterina have long been cherished havens for artists, poets, and travelers seeking inspiration amidst their natural beauty and cultural richness. Legends speak of ancient civilizations that revered these coastal treasures as sacred, leaving behind traces of their existence in ancient ruins and maritime traditions. Stories of love and adventure intertwine with the gentle lapping of waves, whispered by locals who have safeguarded their heritage for generations. Today, they remain enduring symbols of Puglia's maritime heritage and coastal charm, inviting you to discover their hidden stories and create your own cherished memories along their sun-drenched shores.

Figure 2.8: A Typical Sunset in Santa Caterina

47

2.5 Porto Selvaggio

Description:

Tucked away along the rugged coastline of Puglia, Porto Selvaggio captivates with its pristine beauty and untamed charm. The azure waters of the Adriatic Sea gently caress secluded coves and rocky cliffs, while ancient olive trees stand sentinel over sun-drenched pathways that wind through fragrant Mediterranean maquis. The air is perfumed with the scent of wildflowers and saltwater, creating a serene atmosphere that invites exploration and contemplation.

Figure 2.9: The Torre D'Alto In Porto Selvaggio

How to find it:

Discovering Porto Selvaggio is a journey through nature's untouched splendor, following coastal trails that lead from nearby towns or hidden paths through lush forests. As you navigate through the shaded groves of pine and oak trees, the sound of crashing waves grows louder, guiding you to panoramic vistas and hidden alcoves where the sea meets the land. Follow the whispers of the sea breeze and the call of seabirds overhead, leading you to this secluded paradise.

Activities Nearby:

At Porto Selvaggio, immerse yourself in the tranquility of its turquoise waters with a refreshing swim or snorkel, marveling at the vibrant marine life beneath the surface. Explore rugged hiking trails that offer sweeping views of the Adriatic coastline, perfect for capturing breathtaking sunset panoramas. Engage in moments of solitude as you relax on sandy beaches or find shade under ancient olive trees, savoring the simplicity and beauty of this unspoiled coastal sanctuary.

Special Stories From the Past:

Porto Selvaggio has long been a haven for poets, artists, and dreamers drawn to its natural splendor and timeless allure. Legends speak of ancient civilizations that revered this coastal haven as sacred, leaving behind traces of their existence amidst the rocky cliffs and hidden grottoes. Stories of love found and lost echo through its secluded shores, whispered by locals who have safeguarded its secrets for generations. Today, it remains a testament to the enduring power of nature and the profound connection between land and sea, inviting you to uncover its hidden stories and create your own lasting memories in this untouched paradise.

Figure 2.10: The Sun hits Porto Selvaggio

2.6 Grotta del Drago

Description:

Nestled within the rugged cliffs of Puglia's coastline, the Grotta del Drago enchants visitors with its mystical allure and ancient secrets. As you step into its cool, shadowy depths, you are greeted by towering stalactites and stalagmites that seem to guard the cave's inner sanctum. The cavernous chambers echo with the haunting melody of dripping water, carving intricate patterns into the limestone walls over centuries. Sunlight filters through hidden openings, casting ethereal reflections that dance upon the crystal-clear underground pools, revealing glimpses of hidden treasures within.

Figure 2.11: Grotta del Drago, Santa Maria di Leuca

How to find it:

Discovering the Grotta del Drago is a journey through time and nature, following winding paths that wind through olive groves and fragrant Mediterranean flora. Listen for the distant roar of the sea and the whispers of the wind, guiding you to a secluded inlet where the cave's entrance awaits. As you descend into its mysterious depths, the air grows cooler and the scent of earth and saltwater fills your senses, inviting you deeper into this enchanting underworld.

Activities Nearby:

Within the Grotta del Drago, embrace moments of quiet contemplation as you marvel at the natural beauty that surrounds you. Engage in a serene boat ride along the underground river, immersing yourself in the mystical ambiance of the cave's interior. Outside, explore coastal trails that offer panoramic views of the Adriatic Sea, capturing the essence of Puglia's rugged coastline and ancient maritime history. Whether admiring the sunset from a cliffside vantage point or delving into the cave's storied past, the Grotta del Drago offers a glimpse into a world where myth and reality converge.

Special Stories From the Past:

Ancient lore whispers of dragons that once roamed these caverns, their fiery breath shaping the landscape and leaving behind tales of wonder and awe. Over millennia, the Grotta del Drago has served as a sanctuary for ancient civilizations and a source of inspiration for poets and storytellers. Legends of hidden treasures and mythical creatures have woven themselves into the fabric of local folklore, captivating hearts and minds for generations. Today, it remains a testament to the enduring power of nature and the timeless allure of Puglia's hidden wonders, inviting you to uncover its mysteries and forge your own unforgettable story within its ancient walls.

Figure 2.12: The Cliff of the West Pugliese Coast

2.7 Faraglioni di Sant'Andrea

Description:

Rising majestically from the azure waters of the Adriatic Sea, the Faraglioni di Sant'Andrea stand as silent sentinels of nature's enduring beauty. These ancient limestone sea stacks, weathered by wind and waves over millennia, create a dramatic backdrop against the vivid Puglian sky. Their rugged, sheer cliffs rise defiantly from the sea, adorned with lush greenery clinging to their sides, a testament to resilience and timelessness.

Figure 2.13: Faraglioni di Sant'Andrea from the Sea

How to find it:

To witness the Faraglioni di Sant'Andrea in all their splendor, venture along the coastal paths that wind through fragrant pine forests and sun-drenched olive groves. Follow the salty breeze and the rhythmic crashing of waves, guiding you to panoramic viewpoints that offer breathtaking vistas of these natural wonders. As you approach, the sound of seabirds circling above and the distant murmur of the sea below create a symphony of nature's symphony.

Activities Nearby:

At the Faraglioni di Sant'Andrea, embrace the awe-inspiring scenery with leisurely walks along cliffside trails, offering glimpses of secluded coves and pristine beaches below. Capture the perfect photograph as the sun sets behind these iconic formations, painting the sky with hues of gold and crimson. Engage in contemplative moments as you absorb the tranquility of this pristine coastal sanctuary, where time seems to stand still.

Special Stories From the Past:

Legends abound of ancient mariners who navigated by the towering silhouette of the Faraglioni di Sant'Andrea, their distinctive profiles guiding sailors safely home through treacherous waters. Stories of love and loss echo through the ages, whispered by locals who have called these rugged cliffs home for centuries. Today, they remain an enduring symbol of Puglia's natural beauty and cultural heritage, inviting you to discover their timeless allure and create your own story amidst their towering presence.

Figure 2.14: Faraglioni di Sant'Andrea from the Cliff

2.8 Grotta Verde di Andrano

Description:

Hidden along the rugged coastline of Puglia, the Grotta Verde di Andrano beckons with its emerald-hued waters and mysterious caverns carved by the relentless embrace of the Adriatic Sea. Stepping into its cool, dimly lit chambers feels like entering a forgotten realm where time stands still. Sunlight filters through cracks in the cave ceiling, casting ethereal reflections that dance upon the rippling surface of the sea inside, painting the walls with hues of jade and turquoise.

Figure 2.15: The Green Cave, Andrano

How to find it:

Discovering the Grotta Verde di Andrano requires a journey through ancient olive groves and winding coastal paths that wind down to the water's edge. Follow the whispers of the sea breeze and the sound of crashing waves, leading you to a secluded inlet where the cave's entrance awaits. As you descend into its depths, the salty tang of the sea mingles with the earthy aroma of moss-covered rocks, guiding you further into this mesmerizing sanctuary.

Activities Nearby:

At the Grotta Verde di Andrano, immerse yourself in its enchanting waters with a refreshing swim or snorkel, marveling at the hidden wonders beneath the surface. Outside the cave, explore nearby coastal trails that offer panoramic views of cliffs plunging into the azure sea, perfect for capturing breathtaking sunset vistas. Embrace moments of solitude as you listen to the rhythmic lullaby of waves echoing within the cavern, a symphony of nature's serene beauty.

Special Stories From the Past:

Legend whispers of ancient sailors and fishermen who sought shelter within the Grotta Verde di Andrano during treacherous storms, finding solace in its protective embrace. Tales of mermaids and sea nymphs weaving through its labyrinthine passages have enchanted generations, weaving a tapestry of mythical lore that echoes through the ages. Today, it remains a cherished haven where echoes of the past intertwine with the timeless rhythm of the sea, inviting you to uncover its secrets and create your own story amidst its storied depths.

Figure 2.16: Inside the Green Cave, Andrano

2.9 Cava di Bauxite

Description:

Nestled in the heart of Salento, the Cava di Bauxite is a striking and surreal landscape that captivates visitors with its vivid colors and unique geological formations. The abandoned bauxite quarry, once a bustling site of industrial activity, has transformed into a natural wonder, where the deep red hues of the earth contrast sharply with the vibrant greens of surrounding vegetation and the brilliant blue of a small lake that has formed in the quarry basin. This extraordinary site offers a glimpse into the raw beauty and resilience of nature, reclaiming what was once taken by industry and turning it into a place of awe and inspiration.

Figure 2.17: The Wonderful Cava di Bauxite close to Castro and Otranto

How to find it:

The Cava di Bauxite is located near the town of Otranto, in the province of Lecce. To reach this hidden gem, take the SP87 road from Otranto towards the Cape of Otranto, the easternmost point of Italy. A small signpost along the way marks the entrance to the quarry, from where a short walk through a pathway leads you to the breathtaking site. The path is accessible and well-trodden, making it an easy excursion for visitors of all ages.

Activities Nearby:

While visiting the Cava di Bauxite, take the opportunity to explore the rich surroundings of Otranto and its environs. Just a short drive away, you can visit the stunning Otranto Cathedral, known for its exquisite mosaic floor depicting the Tree of Life. The nearby coastline offers numerous pristine beaches and coves, perfect for a relaxing day by the sea. For those seeking adventure, hiking trails along the coastal cliffs provide panoramic views of the Adriatic Sea and lead to the historic Torre del Serpe, an ancient watchtower that stands as a sentinel over the coastline.

Special Stories From the Past:

The Cava di Bauxite holds stories of its industrial past, where, from the 1940s until the 1970s, it was a key site for the extraction of bauxite, an ore used in the production of aluminum. Workers toiled in this quarry, contributing to the economic development of the region. As industry moved on, nature began to reclaim the site, filling the abandoned pit with rainwater to create the small lake that now shimmers at its center. Today, the Cava di Bauxite stands as a testament to the enduring power of nature to heal and transform, turning a once-exploited land into a place of stunning natural beauty and tranquility.

Figure 2.18: The Vivid Red of the Bauxite

Chapter 3: The Most Iconic Pugliese Foods

3.1 Taieddrha

Origins and Cultural Significance

Taieddrha, also known as Tiella di Cozze e Patate, is a traditional dish from the coastal areas of Puglia, particularly popular in the Salento region. This dish has deep roots in local culinary traditions, showcasing the region's rich seafood and agricultural heritage. The name "Taieddrha" is derived from the local dialect, emphasizing its cultural significance as a beloved regional specialty.

Preparation and Ingredients

To prepare Taieddrha, fresh mussels (cozze) and thinly sliced potatoes (patate) are layered with tomatoes, garlic, parsley, and olive oil in a round or oval baking dish. The dish is then covered and baked until the mussels open and release their flavorful juices, infusing the potatoes with seafood essence. This method of cooking ensures that the flavors meld together perfectly, creating a satisfying and aromatic dish.

Traditional Serving and Pairing

Taieddrha is traditionally served as a main course, accompanied by crusty bread to soak up the savory juices. It pairs wonderfully with a crisp white wine from Puglia, enhancing the flavors of the seafood and potatoes. This dish is a testament to the region's bounty from both land and sea, offering a delightful taste of Puglian culinary traditions.

3.2   Panzerotto and Calzone

Origins and Cultural Significance

Panzerotto and Calzone are iconic dishes in Puglian cuisine, cherished for their delicious fillings and crispy fried or baked dough. Panzerotto, originating from Southern Italy and popular in Puglia, is a smaller version of Calzone. These stuffed pastries have roots in Italian culinary tradition dating back centuries. They were originally a way to use up leftover ingredients, making them practical and flavorful additions to local cuisine. Generally, above Brindisi it is called Panzerotto, while in the province of Lecce is called Calzone.

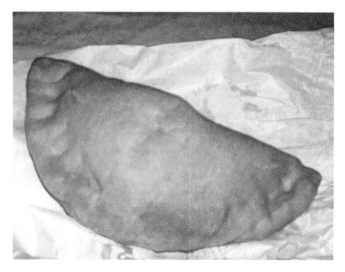

Figure 3.1: Calzone (Lecce) or Panzerotto (elsewhere)

Preparation and Ingredients

To prepare Panzerotto or Calzone, dough is rolled out and filled with a variety of ingredients such as mozzarella, tomato sauce, ricotta, and sometimes cured meats or vegetables. The dough is then folded over the filling, creating a half-moon shape, and either fried until golden and crispy or baked until the dough is lightly browned and cooked through. Each region in Puglia may have its own variations in fillings and cooking methods, but the essence of these dishes lies in the balance of textures and flavors.

59

Traditional Serving and Pairing

Panzerotto or Calzone is typically served hot and fresh, either as a snack or a main dish. It pairs well with a variety of accompaniments such as fresh salads, pickled vegetables, or a glass of local Puglian wine. This hearty dish satisfies both as a quick bite on the go and as a comforting meal enjoyed with family and friends.

3.3 Mozzarella Fior di Latte

Origins and Cultural Significance

Mozzarella Fior di Latte, often simply referred to as Fior di Latte, is a fresh cheese that originated in southern Italy, including Puglia. The name translates to "flower of the milk," highlighting its delicate and creamy texture derived from cow's milk. This cheese holds a special place in Puglian cuisine, where it is used in various dishes ranging from salads to pizzas.

Production and Characteristics

Mozzarella Fior di Latte is made by heating cow's milk and adding rennet to coagulate the milk. The curds are then stretched and kneaded to achieve its characteristic smooth and elastic texture. The cheese is typically shaped into balls or braids and stored in brine to preserve its freshness. It is known for its mild flavor and ability to melt beautifully when heated.

Traditional Use and Pairing

Mozzarella Fior di Latte is a versatile cheese used in both hot and cold dishes. It is a key ingredient in Caprese salad, where it is paired with fresh tomatoes, basil, and extra virgin olive oil. It also tops Neapolitan-style pizzas and is enjoyed on its own with crusty bread and prosciutto. This cheese epitomizes the simplicity and richness of Puglian dairy traditions.

3.4 Panino con i Pezzetti di Cavallo

Origins and Cultural Significance

Panino con i Pezzetti di Cavallo, also known as "Pezzetti di Cavallo," is a traditional sandwich from Puglia, particularly popular in Lecce and the surrounding areas. The name translates to "sandwich with small pieces of horse meat," reflecting its origins as a local street food specialty. Historically, horse meat was a common ingredient due to its availability and affordability, although today other meats like beef or pork may also be used. A song "Mieru Pezzetti and Cazzotti" is dedicated to the football team of Lecce and this special dish.

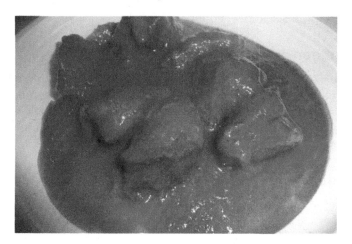

Figure 3.2: Panino con Pezzetti di Cavallo al Sugo

Preparation and Ingredients

To prepare Panino con i Pezzetti di Cavallo, small pieces of meat are marinated with garlic, herbs, and olive oil, then skewered and grilled or pan-fried until tender and flavorful. The meat is typically served in a crusty roll or focaccia bread, along with grilled vegetables such as bell peppers and onions. The sandwich may be dressed with a squeeze of lemon juice or a drizzle of extra virgin olive oil for added flavor.

Traditional Serving and Pairing

Panino con i Pezzetti di Cavallo is a popular street food enjoyed as a quick and hearty meal. It pairs well with a glass of local Puglian wine, such as Primitivo or Negroamaro, enhancing the savory flavors of the grilled meat and vegetables.

3.5 Polpo a Pignata

Origins and Cultural Significance

Polpo a Pignata is a traditional dish from Puglia, specifically popular in coastal towns where fresh octopus (polpo) is abundant. The name "Polpo a Pignata" refers to the traditional cooking method in which the octopus is slow-cooked in a terracotta pot (pignata) with tomatoes, herbs, garlic, and olive oil. This dish showcases the region's strong ties to the Mediterranean sea and its bounty.

Preparation and Ingredients

To prepare Polpo a Pignata, fresh octopus is cleaned and simmered gently in its own juices along with tomatoes, onions, garlic, and herbs. The slow-cooking process allows the flavors to meld together, resulting in tender octopus infused with rich, savory aromas. The dish is typically served with crusty bread to soak up the flavorful sauce.

Traditional Serving and Pairing

Polpo a Pignata is served hot as a main course, often accompanied by a glass of local Puglian white wine, such as Verdeca or Fiano. The wine's crisp acidity complements the dish's robust flavors, enhancing the dining experience.

Figure 3.3: Cooking Octopus

3.6   Peperoni Sott'Aceto con Pangrattato

Origins and Cultural Significance

Peperoni Sott'Aceto con Pangrattato, which translates to "Peppers in Vinegar with Breadcrumbs," is a traditional dish from Puglia that showcases the region's culinary creativity and preservation techniques. This dish is a popular antipasto or side dish, especially during the summer months when peppers are plentiful and at their peak.

Preparation and Ingredients

To prepare Peperoni Sott'Aceto con Pangrattato, bell peppers are roasted or grilled until charred, then peeled and marinated in vinegar with garlic, herbs, and olive oil. The addition of breadcrumbs (pangrattato) adds texture and absorbs the flavors of the marinade, creating a savory and tangy dish. This method of preserving peppers allows them to be enjoyed throughout the year.

Traditional Serving and Pairing

Peperoni Sott'Aceto con Pangrattato is served cold or at room temperature as part of an antipasto platter or alongside grilled meats and seafood. It pairs well with a crisp white wine from Puglia, such as Vermentino or Greco, enhancing the dish's refreshing flavors. This dish exemplifies Puglia's tradition of using simple, fresh ingredients to create vibrant and flavorful dishes.

3.7   Cozze Crude and Ricci di Mare

Origins and Cultural Significance

Cozze Crude and Ricci di Mare are iconic seafood dishes from Puglia, celebrated for their freshness and flavors straight from the Adriatic Sea. These dishes exemplify Puglia's rich maritime heritage and the region's passion for fresh seafood.

Preparation and Ingredients

Cozze Crude consists of fresh raw mussels, carefully cleaned and served on ice or chilled seawater to maintain their freshness. Ricci di Mare, or sea urchins, are opened to reveal their delicate roe, which is enjoyed fresh with a squeeze of lemon juice or drizzled with olive oil. Both dishes highlight the natural flavors of the sea with minimal preparation.

Traditional Serving and Pairing

Cozze Crude and Ricci di Mare are typically served as appetizers or starters, showcasing the bounty of the Adriatic. They are enjoyed with crusty bread to soak up the briny juices and are often paired with a chilled glass of local Puglian white wine, such as Verdeca or Fiano, to complement their fresh and delicate flavors. These dishes capture the essence of Puglian coastal cuisine, offering a taste of the sea in every bite.

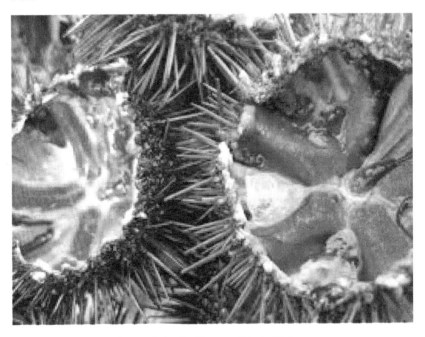

Figure 3.4: The Famous Ricci di Mare

3.8 Orecchiette con Cime di Rape

Origins and Cultural Significance

Orecchiette con Cime di Rape is a quintessential dish from Puglia, celebrated for its simplicity and robust flavors. The name translates to "little ears with turnip tops," referring to the pasta's shape and the bitter leafy greens that accompany it. This dish embodies the agricultural roots of Puglian cuisine, showcasing locally grown ingredients.

Preparation and Ingredients

To prepare Orecchiette con Cime di Rape, orecchiette pasta is cooked until al dente and tossed with sautéed cime di rape (turnip greens) that have been cooked with garlic, chili pepper, and extra virgin olive oil. The bitterness of the greens contrasts beautifully with the slight chewiness of the pasta, creating a harmonious balance of flavors and textures.

Traditional Serving and Pairing

Orecchiette con Cime di Rape is traditionally served as a primo piatto (first course) in Puglia, often garnished with grated pecorino cheese and a drizzle of olive oil. It pairs perfectly with a glass of local Puglian red wine, such as Primitivo or Negroamaro, which complements the dish's hearty flavors. This dish exemplifies Puglian culinary tradi

Figure 3.5: Orecchiette con Cime di Rapa

Chapter 4: The Finest Selection of Wines

4.1 Salice Salentino

History

Salice Salentino, originating from the Salice Salentino DOC area in the Salento peninsula of Puglia, has a long history rooted in ancient winemaking traditions. The wine is primarily crafted from the indigenous Negroamaro grape, known for its deep color and complex flavors.

Production Area

Salice Salentino wines are produced in the Salice Salentino DOC zone, encompassing the towns of Salice Salentino and Veglie. The vineyards here benefit from the region's Mediterranean climate, with hot summers and mild winters, along with the unique "terra rossa" soil rich in iron oxide. These factors contribute to the wine's distinctive character and balanced acidity.

Tasting Notes

Salice Salentino wines typically display a deep ruby-red color with aromas of blackberries, cherries, and hints of spices and herbs. On the palate, they are well-structured with firm tannins and a slightly bitter note that adds to their complexity. The wine pairs excellently with grilled meats, aged cheeses, and traditional Puglian cuisine.

Alcohol by Volume (ABV): Typically ranges from 12.5% to 14%.

4.2 Primitivo di Manduria

History:

Primitivo di Manduria, originating from the town of Manduria in the province of Taranto, Puglia, has a storied history dating back centuries. The Primitivo grape, genetically identical to California's Zinfandel, thrives in the warm Mediterranean climate and fertile soils of this region. Historically, this grape variety was cherished by local farmers for its early ripening characteristics and robust flavors.

Production Area

Primitivo di Manduria is exclusively produced in the heart of the Manduria DOC (Denominazione di Origine Controllata) area, located in the Salento peninsula of southern Puglia. The vineyards here benefit from a unique combination of factors including rich, red soils known locally as "terra rossa," ample sunshine, and cooling sea breezes from the nearby Ionian Sea. These conditions impart distinctive characteristics to the grapes, resulting in wines that are rich in flavor and deeply expressive of their terroir.

Figure 4.1: One of Finest Primitivo di Manduria

Tasting Notes

Primitivo di Manduria wines are characterized by their deep ruby-red color and intense aromas of ripe red berries, plums, and spices. On the palate, they are full-bodied with rich flavors of dark fruits, chocolate, and a hint of vanilla. Velvety tannins and a long, lingering finish make this wine a perfect complement to hearty dishes such as grilled meats, pasta with rich sauces, and aged cheeses.

Alcohol by Volume (ABV): Typically ranges from 14% to 16%.

4.3 Nero di Troia

History

Nero di Troia, also known simply as Troia, is a distinguished red wine originating from the northern part of Puglia. The wine takes its name from the ancient Apulian city of Troy, reflecting its historical roots dating back to Roman times. Nero di Troia is crafted from the indigenous Nero di Troia grape variety, known for its deep color and complex aromas.

Production Area

Nero di Troia grapes thrive in the hilly terrain and calcareous soils of the Castel del Monte DOC area, located near the town of Andria. This region benefits from a continental climate with hot summers and cold winters, contributing to the grape's optimal ripening conditions and the wine's characteristic structure.

Tasting Notes

Nero di Troia wines are characterized by their deep garnet color and intense aromas of dark berries, violets, and spices. On the palate, they exhibit robust tannins and a well-balanced acidity, with flavors of black cherry, plum, and a touch of earthiness. This wine pairs exceptionally well with roasted meats, game dishes, and aged cheeses.

Alcohol by Volume (ABV): Typically ranges from 12.5% to 14%.

4.4 Castel del Monte Rosso Riserva

History

Castel del Monte Rosso Riserva is a prestigious red wine from the Castel del Monte DOC area in Puglia, named after the iconic medieval castle built by Emperor Frederick II. This wine reflects centuries of winemaking tradition and the historical legacy of the region.

Production Area

Located in the hills near Andria, the Castel del Monte DOC area enjoys a unique microclimate and calcareous soils, which impart distinct characteristics to the Aglianico and Nero di Troia grapes used in this wine. The vineyards, set against the backdrop of the majestic castle, evoke a sense of timeless beauty and history.

Tasting Notes

Castel del Monte Rosso Riserva wines are deeply aromatic, with complex layers of dark berries, spices, and hints of earthiness. They boast a robust structure with firm tannins and a velvety texture, showcasing the full potential of the Aglianico and Nero di Troia grapes. Each sip reveals a story of craftsmanship and dedication, making it an experience to be savored with rich Italian dishes or shared moments of celebration.

Alcohol by Volume (ABV): Typically ranges from 13% to 14.5%.

4.5   Bombino Bianco

History

Bombino Bianco is a traditional white wine originating from southern Italy, particularly cultivated in Puglia and neighboring regions. This ancient grape variety has been prized for centuries for its fresh and crisp character.

Production Area

Bombino Bianco thrives in the coastal vineyards of Puglia, where sandy soils and maritime influences create optimal growing conditions. The region's warm climate ensures the grapes reach full ripeness while retaining their vibrant acidity.

Tasting Notes

Bombino Bianco wines are pale straw-yellow in color with delicate aromas of citrus fruits, green apple, and white flowers. On the palate, they are light-bodied and refreshing, with a lively acidity and a clean, dry finish. This versatile wine pairs well with seafood, light pasta dishes, and fresh salads.

Alcohol by Volume (ABV): Typically ranges from 11% to 13%.

4.6 Negroamaro

History

Negroamaro, a dark and rich red wine, has deep roots in Puglian winemaking tradition. It is crafted from the indigenous Negroamaro grape, known for its robust flavors and deep color.

Production Area

Negroamaro grapes are primarily grown in the Salento peninsula of southern Puglia. The region's warm climate and fertile "terra rossa" soils contribute to the grape's richness and intensity.

Tasting Notes

Negroamaro wines exhibit aromas of dark fruits, herbs, and spices, with flavors of black cherry, plum, and hints of cocoa. They have a robust structure with smooth tannins, pairing well with hearty dishes and aged cheeses.

Alcohol by Volume (ABV): Typically ranges from 1.52% to 14%.

Figure 4.2: A Typical Picture of Wine in Glass during Summer

Conclusion and Bonus

As our journey through Puglia draws to a close, we reflect upon the myriad wonders that have unfolded before us. Puglia, with its sun-kissed shores and ancient olive groves, has revealed itself as a land of contrasts and timeless beauty. From the bustling ports of Bari to the serene countryside of Alberobello, each corner of this region offers a glimpse into a rich tapestry of history, culture, and natural splendor.

The heart of Puglia beats with the warmth of its people, whose hospitality has welcomed us into their homes and hearts. Through shared meals of handmade pasta and locally sourced wines, we have experienced the essence of Italian conviviality and the joy of simple pleasures. In every conversation with artisans, farmers, and fishermen, we have witnessed a deep-rooted pride in traditions passed down through generations—a testament to the resilience and spirit of the Pugliese people.

Beyond its tangible beauty and cultural riches, Puglia has left an indelible mark on our souls. It is a land where time seems to stand still amidst ancient olive trees and whitewashed villages, yet where innovation and creativity thrive in bustling cities and artisan workshops. From the mystical caves of Castellana to the timeless elegance of Lecce's Baroque architecture, Puglia's landscapes and landmarks have sparked our imagination and awakened a sense of wonder that will endure long after our journey ends.

In bidding farewell to Puglia, we carry with us not only memories of its sunsets over the Adriatic and fragrant fields of wildflowers but also a deeper appreciation for the interconnectedness of history, culture, and nature. Puglia has taught us the importance of preserving traditions while embracing progress, of cherishing the land that sustains us, and of celebrating the beauty that surrounds us. May our experiences in Puglia inspire us to seek out new adventures, forge meaningful connections, and continue to explore the diverse tapestry of our world with open hearts and minds.

What's Next? Grab Your Free Bonuses!

Step 1

Scan the QR-code or visit the following website:

https://www.lucyevans.shop/puglia-travel-guide-welcome

Step 2:

Leave your data and get access to the bonuses included with any purchase of this book

Step 3:

Leave an honest review on Amazon, your support will make the difference!

Step 4:

Want more of my books? Here a wide selction of lovely crafted books available on Amazon!

Pictures Licenses

Made in the USA
Coppell, TX
01 September 2024